Mean Billy Joe Gill

Joanna Weaver

Illustrated by Tony Kenyon

FaithKidz®
Equipping Kids for Life

An Imprint of Cook Communications Ministries • Colorado Springs, CO

Faith Kidz® is an imprint of Cook Communications Ministries,
Colorado Springs, Colorado 80918
Cook Communications, Paris, Ontario
Kingsway Communications, Eastbourne, England

MEAN BILLY JOE GILL © 2000 by Joanna Weaver for text and Tony Kenyon for illustrations

Editor: Kathy Davis
Graphic Design: Granite Design
First printing, 2000
Manufactured in China
04 03   5 4 3 2

Library of Congress Cataloging-in-Publication Data
Weaver, Joanna.
      Mean Billy Joe Gill/Joanna Weaver ; illustrated by Tony Kenyon
          p. cm. — (Attitude adjusters)
          Summary: Billy is a schoolyard bully, but when he accidentally ruins his own science fair
project, he understands how he makes others feel and learns to live by the Golden Rule.
          ISBN 0-7814-3371-1
          [1. Bullies—Fiction. 2. Christian life—Fiction. 3. Stories in rhyme.]
      I. Kenyon, Tony, ill. II. Title
      PZ8.3.W3797 Bi 2000
      [E]—dc21   99-089820

This book belongs to:

_____

Love,
Joanna Weaver

*"Make sure that nobody pays back
wrong for wrong, but always try to be kind
to each other and to everyone else."*
1 Thessalonians 5:15 (NIV)

Out in the schoolyard, in a corner, on a hill,
stood the king of the playground—Billy Joe Gill.

Each day he would holler
    in the soft morning dew,
A shout to make other
    kids shrink in their shoes:

7

Over and over,
    during recess and lunch,
Billy looked through the playground
    for someone to punch.

He'd push and he'd shove.
He'd steal baseball gloves.
He'd taunt and he'd tease
till kids begged on their knees.

"Oh, Billy, please stop!"
    the crying children said.
But Billy just laughed,
    then bopped 'em on the head.

"You lookin' at me, kid?"
    he'd say with a sneer.
The children would tremble
    and step back in fear.

But when no one was watching,
Billy would sigh.
"It's lonely being me,"
the bully would cry.

But before very long,
        he'd be looking for trouble.
He'd pull a girl's hair,
        pop another kid's bubble.

One Tuesday,
    Billy Joe felt particularly mean,
so he grabbed a small kid
    and started his routine.

But that day in the schoolyard, in a corner, on the sand,
a third-grader named Snittle finally took a stand.
"Billy, you're a bully!" said small Edward Snittle.
And though he looked brave, Edward shook just a little.
"Why do you punch us and throw us to the ground?
How would you feel if we bossed you around?"

The crowd of kids clapped, and one said, "Hooray!"
But Billy just chuckled and went on his way.

"I'd be careful, Edward Snittle,"
Billy said going past.
"You'd better watch out
and you'd better run fast."

The rest of the week,
Billy Joe was unbearable.
He tormented poor Edward
and made his life terrible.

He'd prod and he'd poke.
    He made Edward a joke.
He'd harass and he'd hit,
    till kids begged him to quit.
"Oh, poor Edward Snittle,"
    Billy said with a pout.
"Did I hurt your feelings?
    I said to watch out!"

Then he turned to the counter
    where the science projects sat.
He picked up Edward's rocket
    and gave it a pat.
"You see this?" Billy asked as he
    held the rocket high.
"You may as well kiss your
    science project good-bye!"
"Lift off!" Billy shouted as he
    raced around the room,
tossed the rocket in the air,
    and waited for *kaboom!*
It shattered. It splintered—
    into a million pieces.
But Billy just laughed and
    repeated his thesis:

"I'm the biggest! I'm the best!
    I'm tougher than all the rest.
I'm king of the hill.
    I'm Billy Joe Gill!"
But while Billy was laughing
    and making a scene,
He tripped and fell down
    on a cardboard machine.

"My computer!" howled Billy
    when he saw the destruction.
The simple brown box
    had seen quite a reduction.
It laid there as flat,
    as flat as could be,
so smooshed and so smashed
    there was little left to see.

I need help!

"I worked hard," Billy whined.
    "Now I understand,
why kids get so angry
    when I ruin their plans.
I'm a bully. I'm a mess.
    I'm meaner than all the rest.
I need help! I want help!"
    Billy said with a yelp.

"I'll help you," Edward said
    as he knelt beside Billy.
"Help me?" Billy asked.
    "Why would you? That's silly.
I've been mean, rude, and crude—
    and socially unacceptable."
"I forgive you," Edward said.
    But Billy looked skeptical.
"Come on!" said Edward.
    "I know what to do.
I've got lights, bells, and whistles.
    It'll be just like new!"

Together they worked
    every day after school,
and little by little,
    Billy learned a new rule:
When you do unto others
    what you'd like done to you,
life's sure a lot nicer—
    the Bible is true.
Soon, small Edward Snittle
    and Billy Joe Gill
were friends on the playground
    and friends on the hill.

The rocket and computer
took second and third place.
But it wasn't the ribbons
that put smiles on each face.

GOLDEN RUL

"We may not be the biggest!
    We may not be the best!
But we've found what really matters,
    for we're friends and we are blessed!"

Faith Parenting Guide

I Can Respect Others

Ages: 4-7

Life Issue: I would like my child to fully appreciate others and their possessions.

Spiritual Building Block: Respect

Learning Styles

Sight: Find some old magazines that you and your child can cut up. Look for pictures of people doing something kind (for example, helping others, assisting with house or yard work, reaching out to someone younger or older). Talk about the pictures as you find them. After cutting out the pictures, tape or glue them onto a long piece of cardboard, which you can decorate to look like a ruler. Label it "The Golden Rule," and add a string hanger so your child can put it on a doorknob for a daily reminder to respect others and treat them kindly.

Sound: "Treat others as you want them to treat you," Luke 6:31 (TLB). Explain to your child that Jesus' commandment is often called the Golden Rule. Help your child to memorize this verse. When situations come up where this rule would be helpful (for example, someone's not sharing or someone feels left out), remind your child about the correct response by starting the phrase, "Treat others as . . ." and letting your child finish it.

Touch: Take a "good deed" walk around your home with your child. Bring pencil and paper so you can make a "good deed list." Ask your child to look for projects that need to be done, even simple things such as picking up blocks or toys. Others might include sorting laundry, dusting, sending notes and cards, helping a younger child, and so on. Write down five or more things that your child is able to do, at least as a helper. Talk about how being a helper shows respect for others in your family. Post the list on the refrigerator or other prominent place and check off each good deed as it is finished.